The **Red Badge** of **Courage**

Stephen Crane

Abridged and adapted by Stephen Feinstein

Illustrated by James McConnell

A PACEMAKER CLASSIC

Fearon/Janus/Quercus
Belmont, California

Simon & Schuster Supplementary Education Group

Other Pacemaker Classics

The Adventures of Huckleberry Finn
The Adventures of Tom Sawyer
A Christmas Carol
Crime and Punishment
The Deerslayer
Dr. Jekyll and Mr. Hyde
Ethan Frome
Frankenstein
Great Expectations
Jane Eyre
The Jungle Book
The Last of the Mohicans
Moby Dick
The Moonstone
Robinson Crusoe
The Scarlet Letter
A Tale of Two Cities
The Three Musketeers
The Time Machine
Treasure Island
20,000 Leagues Under the Sea
Two Years Before the Mast
Wuthering Heights

Copyright © 1991 by Fearon/Janus/Quercus, a division of Simon & Schuster Supplementary Education Group, 500 Harbor Boulevard, Belmont, California 94002. All rights reserved. No part of this book may be reproduced by any means, transmitted, or translated into a machine language without written permission from the publisher.

Library of Congress Catalog Card Number: 90-85003

ISBN 0-8224-9356-X

Printed in the United States of America

10 9 8 7 6 5 4 3

Contents

1. New Recruits 1
2. The War Gets Closer 12
3. The Test 17
4. "Where Were You Hit, Boy?" 26
5. Return to the Regiment 34
6. A Second Chance 43
7. "A War Devil" 48
8. "A Lot of Mule Drivers" 55
9. Victory 66
10. Glad to Be Alive 72

1 New Recruits

The cold fog slowly lifted. As the new day began, the army regiment that was camped on the hillside awakened. The young Union soldiers were mostly new recruits. After several months of drilling in camp, they were eager to see action. Last night they had seen the gleam of campfires on hills across the river. Everyone knew they were enemy campfires.

A tall soldier went down to the river to wash a shirt. When he returned, he was very excited.

"We're going to move tomorrow, for sure," he announced to a group of soldiers. "We're going way up the river, cut across, and then we'll come around behind them."

"It's a lie, that's all it is, just a big lie," said another soldier loudly. His smooth face was flushed, and his hands were thrust into his trouser pockets. "I don't believe this old army is ever going to move. We're set. I've gotten ready to move eight times in the past two weeks. And we haven't moved yet."

The tall soldier felt the need to defend the truth of the rumor he had started. He and Wilson, the loud soldier, came close to fighting over it. But they backed down when a corporal walked by.

In the meantime, the rumor was spreading. The whole camp seemed to be discussing the matter. One soldier after another came up to the tall soldier to ask for more information.

"What's up, Jim?"

"The army's going to move," said the tall soldier.

"Ah, what are you talking about? How do you know it is?"

"Well, you can believe me or not, just as you like. It doesn't make any difference to me," said the tall soldier.

The tall soldier, Jim Conklin, seemed so sure of himself that most of the men believed him. The soldiers grew excited as they talked about moving out.

One of them, a youth named Henry Fleming, remained quiet. He was listening very closely to what the other soldiers were saying. They were talking about possible plans of marches and attacks. Of course, nobody knew for sure what orders they would be given.

Finally, Henry had heard enough. He needed to be alone. He got up and walked to his tent. He crawled inside and lay down on his bunk. The sunlight outside made the wall of the tent glow a light yellow shade.

The youth lay there as if in a trance. So they were at last going to fight the Rebels! Tomorrow, perhaps,

2

there would be a battle. And he would be in it. For a time he had to work hard to make himself believe it. He was actually going to take part in one of those great affairs of the earth.

Henry had dreamed of battles all his life. The great bloody wars of his imagination had thrilled him with their sweep and fire. And in his daydreams, Henry had always fought his way through the battles as a mighty hero. But Henry didn't really believe that such battles were possible anymore. They belonged in the distant past, along with heavy crowns and high castles.

When Henry had first heard about the war in his own country, he wasn't sure what to believe. He thought that it must be some sort of a play affair. Men today were too timid for war. Religion and education, he felt, had gotten rid of the killer instinct in men.

But the more news that Henry heard about the war, the more eager he became to enlist. He read reports of marches and conflicts that shook the land. He longed to see it all for himself.

Henry's mother was dead set against his enlisting. She gave him hundreds of reasons why he was more important on the farm than on the field of battle. But almost every day the newspapers gave accounts of a great victory. The gossip in the village was filled with tales of glory.

One night the village church bell started clanging. In the distance, Henry could hear the excited voices of village folk. They were no doubt discussing yet another great battle. It caused Henry to shiver in excitement. His mind was made up. He ran down to his mother's room and said, "Ma, I'm going to enlist."

"Henry, don't you be a fool," his mother had replied. Then she covered her face with the quilt and went back to sleep.

The next morning, however, Henry went to the village. He enlisted in a regiment that was being formed there. When he got home, his mother was milking the cow. "Ma, I've enlisted," he said.

There was a short silence. Finally Henry's mother said, "The Lord's will be done, Henry." Then she continued to milk the cow.

Soon the day came for Henry to leave for the army. He got dressed in his new blue uniform. It was time to say good-bye to his mother. She was busy peeling potatoes. When she looked up at Henry, he could see two tears leaving trails as they rolled down her cheeks.

"You watch out, Henry," she said. She kept on peeling the potatoes as she spoke. "You take good care of yourself in this here fighting business. Don't go thinking you can lick the whole Rebel army at

the start, because you can't. You're just one little fellow among a whole lot of others. You've got to keep quiet and do what they tell you, Henry.

"I've knit you eight pairs of socks, and I've put in all your best shirts. I want my boy to be just as warm and comfortable as anyone in the army. Whenever the socks get holes in them, I want you to send them right back to me so I can fix them.

"And always be careful of the company you keep, Henry. There are lots of bad men in the army. The army makes them wild. They'd like nothing better than to teach a young fellow like you to drink and swear. I don't want you ever to do anything that you would be ashamed of.

"And Henry, you must never do any shirking on my account. If the time comes when you have to do a mean thing or take a chance that might get you killed, don't think of anything except what's right. The Lord will take care of us all.

"Now don't forget about the socks and the shirts, child. And I've put a cup of blackberry jam in your bundle. I know how you like it above all things. Good-bye, Henry. Watch out, and be a good boy."

Henry had gotten a little impatient during his mother's speech. He hadn't quite expected her to say so much, and he was annoyed. He left feeling a sense of relief.

He looked back when he got to the gate. His

mother was kneeling among the potato peels. She was looking up, and her face was stained with tears. Her thin body was shaking. Henry bowed his head and went on, feeling suddenly ashamed of himself.

On the train to Washington, Henry's spirit had soared. His regiment was fed and cheered at station after station. After a while he began to believe that he must be a hero. There were lavish spreads of bread and cold meats, coffee, pickles, and cheese. The girls smiled at him, and the old men patted and complimented him. Henry felt the strength to do mighty deeds growing within him.

After the journey had come months of boring life in a camp. Henry had thought that real war would be a series of death struggles. He imagined there would be little time in between for sleep and meals. But when his regiment had come to the field, it hadn't been that way at all. The army had done little but sit still and try to keep warm. Then the troops were drilled and drilled and reviewed, over and over again.

Now as Henry lay in his bunk, one thought kept going through his mind. On the very next day, he might have to fight in a real battle. How would he act on the battlefield? Somehow he wasn't feeling very much like a hero. In fact, a little bit of panic was growing in him. What if he turned and ran away during the battle?

Henry jumped up from his bunk and paced back and forth. "Good Lord, what's the matter with me!" he said aloud.

Jim Conklin and Wilson came into the tent. They were still arguing.

"That's all right," said the tall soldier. "You don't have to believe me. Pretty soon you'll find out I was right."

Wilson grunted. "Well, you don't know everything in the world, do you?" he said.

Henry stopped pacing and said, "Going to be a battle for sure, is there, Jim?"

"Of course there is," replied the tall soldier. "You just wait till tomorrow, and you'll see one of the biggest battles there ever was."

"Thunder!" said the youth.

"Oh, you'll see fighting this time, my boy. Regular out-and-out fighting," added the tall soldier. He then told them that the cavalry had started to move out that morning.

Henry remained silent for a time. At last he spoke to the tall soldier. "Jim!" he said.

"What?"

"How do you think the regiment will do?"

"Oh, they'll be brave enough all right, once they get into it," said Jim.

"Think any of the boys will run?" asked Henry.

"Well, there may be a few. There are some who

run off in every regiment. Especially when they first go under fire," said Jim.

"Oh, you think you know," began the loud soldier with scorn.

Wilson and Jim began to argue again. Finally Henry interrupted them. "Did you ever think you might run yourself, Jim?" he said.

The tall soldier waved his hand. "Well, if the fighting got too hot, and if a whole lot of boys started to run, I suppose I'd run. And once I started to run, I'd run like the devil. Make no mistake. But if everyone was standing and fighting, why, I'd stand and fight, too. You can bet on it."

"Huh!" said the loud soldier.

Henry was grateful for Jim's words.

The next morning, the soldiers learned that Jim Conklin's rumor had been a mistake. The regiment wasn't going anywhere that day. Some of the men sneered at the tall soldier.

For Henry, this news wasn't a relief at all. It just meant that he would have more time to dwell on his fears. And the worst part of it was that Henry was afraid to tell anybody the truth about how he felt. With each passing day, Henry grew more afraid that he might run from the coming battle.

Then one day soon after, the regiment moved out before the break of dawn. The men marched all day. At times there would be grumbling and arguing. At other times there would be jokes and laughter. But Henry remained silent all day. By nightfall the regiment had set up camp in a field.

Henry wandered off a ways in the darkness. The many campfires, with the black forms of men passing back and forth, gave off strange effects. Henry lay down in the grass. The blades pressed softly against his cheek.

As he lay there in the moonlight, Henry felt sorry for himself. He wished that he were home again. He would have given anything to be making the rounds from the house to the barn. He felt that he was not cut out to be a soldier.

Then Henry heard the rustle of grass. When he turned his head, he saw the loud soldier. He called out, "Oh, Wilson!"

Wilson looked down. "Why, hello, Henry; is it you? What are you doing here?"

"Oh, just thinking," said the youth.

Wilson sat down and lighted his pipe. "You're getting blue, my boy. What's wrong with you?"

"Nothing," said the youth.

Wilson began to talk about the coming battle. "Oh, we've got 'em now! At last, we'll lick them good!" He went on like this for a while. As he spoke he got excited. He got up and paced back and forth.

"Oh, you're going to do great things, I suppose," said Henry.

"I don't know," said Wilson. "I suppose I'll do as well as the rest."

"How do you know you won't run when the time comes?" asked Henry.

"Run?" said the loud soldier. "Run? Of course not!" He laughed.

"Well, lots of good men have thought they were going to do great things before the fight. But then when the time came, they ran," said Henry.

"That's true, I guess. But *I'm* not going to run," said the loud soldier. "The man that bets on my running will lose his money. That's all there is to it."

"Oh, shucks!" said the youth. "You don't think you're the bravest man in the world, do you?"

"No, I don't," said Wilson angrily. "And who are you, anyhow? You talk as if you think you're Napoleon Bonaparte." He glared at the youth for a moment and then walked away.

Now Henry felt more alone than ever. No one else seemed worried. Henry seemed to be the only one wrestling with such a terrible personal problem.

Henry walked slowly back to his tent. He stretched himself out on a blanket by the side of the snoring tall soldier. Henry stared at the reflection of a fire on the wall of his tent for what seemed like hours. Finally he fell asleep.

2 The War Gets Closer

The following night, the regiment was ordered to move out. The column of soldiers filed across two pontoon bridges. Then the men marched along a narrow road through the forest for much of the night. Sometime before dawn they stopped and set up camp.

Early the next morning the soldiers were awakened from a deep sleep. They were ordered to pack up and get moving again. The regiment tramped through the forest all day. At dusk the men set up a new camp. This routine kept up for the next several days. Each night the troops camped in a different place.

One gray dawn, Henry was kicked in the leg by the tall soldier. The next thing the youth knew, he was running along a path in the woods. Henry was not entirely awake yet. On each side of him men were panting and muttering. The shrill voice of Wilson, the loud soldier, could be heard: "What the devil are they in such a hurry for?"

As Henry ran, his canteen banged against his thigh. His backpack bobbed softly, and his rifle bounced from his shoulder at each stride. He was out of breath. How long would they have to run like this, Henry wondered.

As the sun's rays broke through the early morning fog, a sudden burst of gunfire could be heard in the distance. Henry thought that the time had come. He was about to be tested.

Somewhere up ahead, beyond the next hill, artillery began to boom. Henry looked around him. He was completely surrounded by the other troops. He saw that it would be impossible to escape from the regiment. He was in a moving box.

Before long the troops came upon the body of a dead soldier. He lay upon his back staring at the sky. Henry forced himself to look at the dead man's gray face. The man's beard moved in the breeze, as if a hand were stroking it. The regiment slowed down for a moment but kept marching.

A wave of fear swept over Henry. Suddenly everything seemed wrong. The sounds of gunfire up ahead were almost constant now. Why were the generals leading them right to the enemy? The generals were idiots to send them marching into a death trap!

Henry wanted to shout out a warning to the other troops. But he never got the words out. He looked at the men around him. They were calmly marching forward. Henry was afraid they would laugh at his warning. They would jeer at him.

Finally the regiment came to a halt. The men began to build a low wall of stones, earth, and sticks for protection. They were very close to the fighting now. The air was hazy with gunsmoke. Soon the troops were ordered to move to a different position. But just as they were digging in, they were ordered to move once more.

At the third position, the soldiers ate their noon meal. Henry fixed a sandwich of cracker and pork. By this time he was so jumpy that he could hardly swallow the food. He was anxious to begin fighting and find out what was going to happen.

The tall soldier was sitting nearby eating. Henry

went over to him. "Jim," he cried, "I can't stand this much longer. I don't see what good it does to make us wear out our legs for nothing."

The tall soldier looked up at him. "Oh, I suppose we have to keep moving just to keep from getting too close, or something," he said.

Once again the regiment was ordered to move. The column went up a hillside and continued along the top of the ridge. From here, through openings in the trees, Henry could see the battlefield and the flashes of fire from the rifles. Clouds of smoke were moving slowly across the fields.

As Henry crouched down to look at the scene, he felt a heavy hand upon his shoulder. He turned around and saw that it was Wilson, the loud soldier.

"It's my first and last battle, old boy," said Wilson. He was pale, and his lip was trembling. "Something tells me . . ."

"What?" said the youth in astonishment.

"I'm a dead duck this first time and . . . I want you to take these things to my folks." Wilson ended in a sob of pity for himself. He handed Henry a small packet wrapped in a yellow envelope.

"Why, what the devil . . . ?" began the youth again.

But Wilson looked at him with a deathly stare. He raised a limp hand and turned away.

The regiment marched down from the ridge and halted near the edge of a grove of trees. As the men were digging in, a shell came screaming in just above their heads. It exploded as it landed nearby, showering them with brown earth and pine needles.

Now bullets began to whistle among the branches and nip at the trees. Twigs and leaves came sailing down. Henry and the others were constantly dodging and ducking their heads.

Then the lieutenant got shot in the hand. He began to swear so loudly that the whole regiment let out a nervous laugh. It was as if he had hit his fingers with a hammer at home. The captain of the company rushed up. With his sword tucked under his arm, he took out a handkerchief. He began to bind the lieutenant's wound. The two of them argued about how the binding should be done.

Suddenly wild yells came from behind a wall of smoke. A mob of Union soldiers was running toward them. Two mounted officers of this regiment galloped about angrily screaming orders at their men. But the fleeing men paid no attention to them. They swept past Henry's regiment and kept on running.

Henry and the other new recruits grew pale. "My God! Saunders has gotten crushed!" whispered the man at Henry's elbow. Henry hadn't seen whatever it was that caused these men to run. But he was afraid that when he did see, he would run better than the best of them.

3 The Test

The men of Henry's regiment waited in a grove of trees. The next move was up to the enemy. The moments of waiting seemed to go on forever.

For some reason, Henry's thoughts went back to his childhood. He remembered the village street before the arrival of the circus parade. As a small boy he had shared the excitement of the waiting crowd. Henry half expected at any moment to see the circus lady on the white horse ride by. Suddenly someone cried, "Here they come! Here they come!"

Across the smoke-filled fields came a swarm of running men. They were giving shrill yells as they charged. They came on, stooping and swinging their rifles at all angles. A Rebel flag, tilted forward, was near the front of the charge.

In his excitement, Henry couldn't think clearly. He had the awful thought that perhaps his gun was not loaded. He tried to remember the moment when he had loaded it, but he could not.

A hatless Union general galloped up. He pulled his dripping horse to a stop near the colonel. He shook his fist in the other man's face. "You've got to hold them back!" he shouted.

The colonel began to stammer, "A . . . all right, General, all right, by God! We—we'll do our . . . we . . . we'll d . . . d . . . do our best, General!"

The general galloped away, and the colonel began scolding the men. The man at Henry's elbow was mumbling, as if to himself: "Oh, we're in for it now! Oh, we're in for it now!"

The captain of the regiment had been pacing back and forth in the rear. He kept repeating to the men, "Hold your fire, boys. Don't shoot till I tell you. Save your fire. Wait till they get close up. Don't be damned fools."

Sweat streamed down Henry's face. He wiped his eyes with his coat sleeve. His mouth hung slightly open. He stared at the enemy soldiers crossing the field in front of him. They were getting closer.

In an instant, Henry stopped worrying whether or not his rifle was loaded. He raised his gun into position and fired a first wild shot. At that moment gunfire broke out all around him.

Soon Henry was working at his weapon in an automatic way. Over and over again, he would aim, fire, reload, and aim and fire again. It was as if he were a carpenter working as hard as he could at his job. He was too busy to feel afraid.

Henry was sharply aware of his comrades about him. Somehow he felt a strong sense of brotherhood with them. This feeling was much stronger than his feeling for the Union cause. What he felt was the strange brotherhood born of the smoke and danger of death.

After a while, Henry began to feel the effects of the fighting. There was a blistering sweat. His eyeballs felt as if they were about to crack like hot stones. A burning roar filled his ears. And the gunsmoke that was swirling all around seemed to be choking him.

Henry began to feel a red rage. He hated all the noise, smoke, and heat. He hated his rifle because he could only shoot at one soldier at a time. He wished he could wipe out the enemy with one mighty blow.

It was impossible to know exactly what was going on in all the confusion. Some men shouted and swore, others babbled and made strange sounds. There were cheers, snarls, and prayers. The officers were rushing around behind the lines. They were roaring directions at the tops of their lungs.

Here and there, men dropped like bundles. The captain of Henry's regiment had been killed right at the start. His body lay stretched out on the ground in the position of a tired man resting. His face looked astonished and sad.

The man right next to Henry was grazed by a shot. Blood streamed down his face. He clapped both hands to his head. "Oh!" he said, and ran.

Another man grunted suddenly as if he had been struck by a club in the stomach. He sat down and gazed ahead.

Farther up the line a man standing behind a tree had his knee joint splintered. Immediately he dropped his rifle and gripped the tree with both arms. And there he remained, clinging and crying for help.

At last an excited yell went up along the line. The firing died down to a few pops. As the smoke slowly drifted away, Henry saw that the charge had been beaten back. The enemy had retreated.

Up and down the line, men were saying, "Well, we've held them back; darned if we haven't." The men smiled at one another.

Henry turned to look behind him and off to both sides. He saw a few motionless forms on the ground. They lay twisted in fantastic positions. Arms were bent and heads were turned in horrible ways. It looked as if the dead men had been dumped upon the ground from the sky.

Henry took a long swallow of warm water from his canteen. Now the day was peaceful and quiet, except for the sound of gunfire far off in the distance. Henry noticed the pure blue sky and the sun shining on the trees and fields. It seemed surprising that nature had been calmly going about her business in the midst of such horror.

So it was all over at last! The supreme test had been passed. Henry reviewed the battle in his mind. He was feeling very pleased with himself. He had indeed proved to be a fine, brave soldier.

Henry shook hands with some of the soldiers. Men smiled happily. But while they were congratulating one another, cries of amazement suddenly broke out. "Here they come again!" someone shouted. "Here they come again!"

The youth turned his eyes quickly toward the field. He saw masses of men running toward them out of a distant woods. Henry stared ahead in disbelief. Again he saw the tilted Confederate flag speeding forward.

Shells came swirling again, exploding in the grass or among the trees. Surely, Henry thought, this impossible thing was not about to happen. He waited as if he expected the enemy to suddenly stop, apologize, and retreat. He wanted to hear that it was all a mistake.

Firing began somewhere in the regiment and ripped along the line in both directions. The level sheets of flame sent up great clouds of smoke. As the exhausted men swung into action, Henry grabbed his rifle and joined them.

Henry slowly lifted his rifle and tried to see through the smoke. He caught views of the field covered with running and yelling men.

The youth was so exhausted that the muscles of his arms felt numb and bloodless. His hands felt clumsy and too large, as if he were wearing invisible mittens. In his thoughts, he began to exaggerate the strength, skill, and bravery of the enemy soldiers. They must be machines of steel. It would be impossible to stop them.

A soldier near Henry, who had been working hard at his rifle, suddenly stopped. Then he turned and ran, howling as he fled. Soon another man also threw down his gun and fled. There was no shame on his face, but only fear. He ran like a rabbit.

Others began to scamper away through the smoke. The youth saw the few fleeting forms. It seemed to him as if the regiment were leaving him behind. He heard himself yelling with fright. Then he swung about and began to speed toward the rear.

He ran like a blind man. Two or three times he fell down. He didn't even notice that his rifle and cap were gone. His unbuttoned coat flapped in the wind. His canteen swung out behind him.

After turning his back on the fight, Henry's thoughts went wild. He was sure that death was about to thrust him between the shoulder blades. Now he was only dimly aware of men on his right and left. It seemed to him that all the regiment was fleeing. On his face was a look of horror at the things he was imagining.

Once some shells came hurtling over Henry's head with long wild screams. He imagined them to have rows of cruel teeth that grinned at him. One shell exploded right in front of him. Henry threw himself on the ground. Then he sprang up and went crashing through some bushes.

As the youth ran, he was forced to change direction many times. After a while, he lost his sense of direction.

Henry came to a small clearing in the woods. He could see a general on horseback surrounded by several other horsemen. Another officer on horseback approached the group.

After a moment, the general bounced excitedly in his saddle. "Yes, by heavens, they've held them!" he roared at his staff. "We'll wallop them now. We've got them for sure."

Henry's heart sank. He knew the general was talking about his regiment. So they had held the line after all! There had been no retreat. A wave of shame washed over Henry. He wondered what his comrades would say when he appeared in camp. In his mind he heard their howls and jeers.

The longer the youth thought about his regiment, the angrier he got. After all, he had done the smart thing—the right thing. Since the regiment was about to be destroyed, he was *right* to try and save himself. That's what each of his comrades should have done as well.

Every soldier was a little piece of the regiment. It was the duty of all these little pieces to save themselves. Then, later on, the officers could put all the little pieces back together again. In this way, Henry reasoned, there would still be a regiment. And they would fight again another day.

Henry began to pity himself. How could he ever return to his regiment? What could he say to the men? They wouldn't understand him. He fled deeper into the thick woods, as if he wanted to bury himself.

After a time the sounds of rifles grew faint, and the cannon boomed in the distance. Henry came to a small open space in the dark gloomy woods. He stopped suddenly in horror. Seated with his back against a tree was a dead man. The corpse was dressed in a uniform that had once been blue.

The eyes, staring at the youth, looked like those of a dead fish. The mouth was open. Little ants ran over the gray skin of the face. One was carrying some sort of a bundle along the upper lip. The dead man and the living one exchanged a long look.

Henry turned and fled through the underbrush. Branches pushed against him. His feet caught in the shrubs. In his mind was a picture of the black ants swarming over the gray face. The ants were moving closer to the dead man's eyes.

4 "Where Were You Hit, Boy?"

The sun sank until slanted bronze rays struck the forest. As Henry ran through the trees, he tried to sort out his feelings. One moment he wished to be miles away. The next moment he wanted to see what was happening on the battlefield.

Henry slowed down. Then he stopped to listen. All around him it was quiet, except for the sounds of the insects. Now and then, he could still hear cracks of gunfire in the distance. Henry began walking quickly. He was eager to reach the edge of the forest.

Finally Henry came to a road. A blood-stained crowd of soldiers went streaming by. The wounded men were cursing, groaning, and wailing. They were heading away from the battlefield.

Henry stood there and watched. He saw an officer being carried along by two privates. The wounded man was angry. "Don't joggle so, Johnson, you fool," he cried. "You think my leg is made of iron? If you can't carry me carefully, put me down and let someone else do it."

One of the wounded men had a shoeful of blood. He hopped along like a schoolboy in a game. He

26

was laughing in a strange way. Another man was swearing at the general and blaming him for his wounds.

Henry joined this crowd and marched along with it. A tattered man limped along quietly at Henry's side. He was covered with dust, blood, and powder stains from his hair to his shoes. Henry noticed that the tattered soldier had two wounds, one in the head and one in the arm. His head was bound with a blood-soaked rag. And his wounded arm dangled like a broken tree limb. After they had walked for some time, the tattered man spoke to Henry.

"It was a pretty good fight, wasn't it?" the man said.

"Yes," said the youth shortly. He walked faster, but the tattered soldier kept up with him.

"It was a pretty good fight, wasn't it?" the man repeated. "Darned if I ever saw fellows fight so well. I knew it would turn out this way. You can't lick these tough Yankee boys. No, sir! They're real fighters, they are. Not one of them ran away once the fighting started."

He glanced at Henry, but the youth looked straight ahead and said nothing. Then the tattered man asked in a brotherly tone, "Where were you hit, boy?"

Henry felt instant panic at this question. "What?" he asked.

"Where were you hit?" repeated the tattered man.

"Why," Henry began, "I wasn't . . . that is . . . I . . . " He turned away suddenly and slid through the crowd. The tattered man looked after him in astonishment. Henry fell back in the column of men until the tattered man was not in sight. Then the youth walked on with the others.

Henry's face was flushed. Because of the tattered man's question, he now felt that his shame could be seen by all. He kept glancing at the wounded men on each side of him. Could they see his guilt? Many of the men were bleeding. Henry envied their torn bodies. He wished that he, too, had a wound— a red badge of courage.

In the crowd ahead, Henry noticed a tall man who moved along stiffly. He had been badly wounded. His tight lips seemed to be holding back moans of great pain. Something about him looked familiar to Henry. Suddenly, the youth gave a start, as if he had been bitten. He went forward and laid a shaky hand on the tall soldier's arm.

"God! Jim Conklin!" the youth gasped.

The tall soldier turned a gray face toward Henry. "Hello, Henry," he said.

The youth felt wobbly and he stared strangely. He stuttered and stammered. "Oh, Jim . . . Jim . . . oh, Jim . . ."

The tall soldier held out his bloody hand. "Where you been, Henry?" he asked. "I thought maybe you got killed. You know, I got shot out there. Yes, I got shot." He repeated this fact as if he didn't know how it had come about.

The two friends marched on. Suddenly, the tall soldier seemed to be overcome by terror. He grabbed the youth's arm. Then he began to speak in a shaking whisper. "I tell you what I'm afraid of, Henry. I'm afraid I'll fall down. And then, you know, those damned artillery wagons will run over me. That's what I'm afraid of." His eyes rolled wildly in terror.

"I'll take care of you, Jim," cried the youth. "You can count on me. Here, let me help you. Come on, lean on me."

But the tall soldier suddenly seemed to forget his fears. He brushed Henry aside saying, "No . . . no . . . leave me be." He moved ahead, and Henry had to follow.

Soon Henry heard a voice talking over his shoulder. Turning around, he saw that the voice belonged to the tattered soldier. "You'd better get that man out of the way, partner. There's a battery coming fast down the road. He'll get run over. He'll be gone in five minutes, anyhow . . . you can see that. But you better get him out of the road. Where the blazes is he getting the strength to keep going?"

"Lord knows!" cried the youth.

Henry ran forward and grasped the tall soldier by the arm. "Jim! Jim!" he said. "Come with me."

"Huh," the tall soldier said weakly. He stared at the youth for a moment. At last he spoke as if he dimly understood. "Oh! Into the fields? Oh!"

The tall soldier stumbled blindly through the grass. He was running in a kind of zigzag line toward a clump of bushes.

Just then the artillery battery came racing down the road. Henry and the tattered soldier chased after Jim. When they caught up with him, Henry said, "Jim, what are you doing? Where are you going? You'll hurt yourself."

Jim turned and faced Henry. "Don't touch me. Leave me be, can't you? Leave me be for a minute."

The tall soldier ran ahead again. Henry and the tattered soldier tried to keep up with him. Then they saw him stop and stand still.

"Jim," Henry cried.

"Leave me be," said the tall soldier. He stared into space. Then his chest began to heave. His eyes rolled and his legs began to shake. Finally his body seemed to stiffen. He began to tip forward, slow and straight, like a falling tree. His left shoulder struck the ground first.

Henry rushed over to his fallen friend. He gazed on the man's deathly pale face. Jim's mouth was open and his teeth were bared in a terrible smile. The flap of Jim's blue jacket had fallen away from his body. The man's side looked as if it had been chewed by wolves.

The youth turned with sudden rage toward the battlefield. He shook his fist. "Hell—" he cried. He threw himself down on the ground.

The tattered man looked at the corpse. He said, "Well, he's gone, isn't he? Nobody will bother him now. We better think about ourselves. I must say I'm not feeling so great myself."

Henry looked up at him. The man's face was turning blue. "Good Lord!" Henry cried. "You're not going to . . . not you, too."

The tattered man waved his hand. "Not me. Well, there's no use in our staying here. He can't tell us anything now."

They turned their backs on the corpse and walked away. They crossed the field slowly and silently.

"I don't believe I can walk much farther," said the tattered soldier at last. "You look pretty worn out yourself. I bet you've got a worse wound than you think. You better take care of it. It doesn't do to let such things go. Now where were you hit?"

The youth made an angry motion with his hand. "Don't bother me," he said.

32

"Well, Lord knows I don't want to bother anybody," said the man.

The youth had been struggling with his feelings. Now he glanced with hatred at the tattered man. "Good-bye," he said in a hard voice.

The tattered man looked at him in amazement. "Why, partner, where are you going?" he said.

"Over there," said Henry, pointing across the field.

"Well, now, look here, this won't do," said the tattered man. His head was hanging forward now. His words were not clear. "It's not right for you . . . to go tramping off . . . with a bad hurt . . . it's not right."

Henry climbed over a fence and started out across the field. He knew he should stay with the tattered soldier. The man was probably going to die. But the man's simple and kindly questions had been like knife thrusts to Henry. He had to get away.

The youth went on. Just once, he turned to look back. He saw the tattered man wandering about helplessly in the field.

5 Return to the Regiment

The roar of the battle was growing louder. Great clouds of brown smoke floated high up in the air. When Henry came around the side of a small hill, he saw the road again. Now it was filled with a crowd of wagons, teams, and men. Fear was sweeping all of them along.

The youth watched as the cracking whips bit and the horses plunged and tugged. The white-topped wagons stumbled along like fat white sheep. Men were shouting commands and curses.

This sight made Henry feel happy. Everyone seemed to be retreating. Perhaps, then, he was not so bad after all. But his good feelings did not last long. Soon, a column of soldiers came into view. They were heading toward the battle.

These soldiers were moving quickly. They forced their way through parts of the crowd that was fleeing. Their commands to make way had the ring of great importance. After all, they were rushing forward to meet the enemy. Nothing mattered as long as they got to the front on time.

As Henry watched these brave men, a black cloud fell over him again. If only he could be like them!

If only he could feel the way they seemed to feel! These men were true heroes. The music of the tramping feet, the sharp voices, and clanking rifles filled him with excitement.

Henry wondered whether he could march into battle with these brave men. But how could he? He no longer had his rifle. But he could probably find one. And what about his regiment? It would be a miracle if he could find them in all the confusion. But he *could* fight with *any* regiment.

The more Henry thought about it, the worse he felt. He couldn't join these men. He wasn't like them at all. He could never be a hero. After all, he had fled during the battle. And now he was *afraid* of finding his regiment, even if it were possible. The men would ask him what happened. And he would have to invent some lies. They would see right through him. Everybody would know that he was a coward.

Henry groaned from his heart and went staggering off. As he slowly crossed a field, he became aware of a terrible thirst. His face was so dry that he thought he could feel his skin crackle. Each bone of his body had an ache in it. His feet were like two sores. And his body was crying out for food. There was a dull, heavy feeling in his stomach.

The blue haze of evening was upon the field. The lines of the forest cast long purple shadows. One cloud lay along the red western sky. For some time Henry had listened to the distant booming of the artillery. Now he heard the guns suddenly roar out. He imagined them shaking in black rage.

Henry stopped and watched as blue smoke curled and clouded above the treetops. Through the thickets he could sometimes see a distant pink glare. Suddenly Henry saw dark waves of men come sweeping out of the woods. They charged across the field toward him. Soon they were leaping and scampering all about him.

The youth was filled with amazement. Were these those same brave soldiers he had watched just moments before? He tried to ask them what had happened. But they paid no attention to him as they fled by. They did not even seem to see him.

Finally Henry grabbed a man by the arm. They swung around face to face.

"Why . . . why . . . " stammered the youth.

The man screamed, "Let go of me! Let go of me!" He was heaving and panting and his eyes were rolling. He still grasped his rifle. Henry wouldn't let go of him, and he was dragged along several paces.

"Let go of me! Let go of me!" the man shouted.

"Why . . . why . . . " Henry stuttered.

"Well, then!" shouted the man in a rage. He swung his rifle. It crashed upon the youth's head. The man ran on.

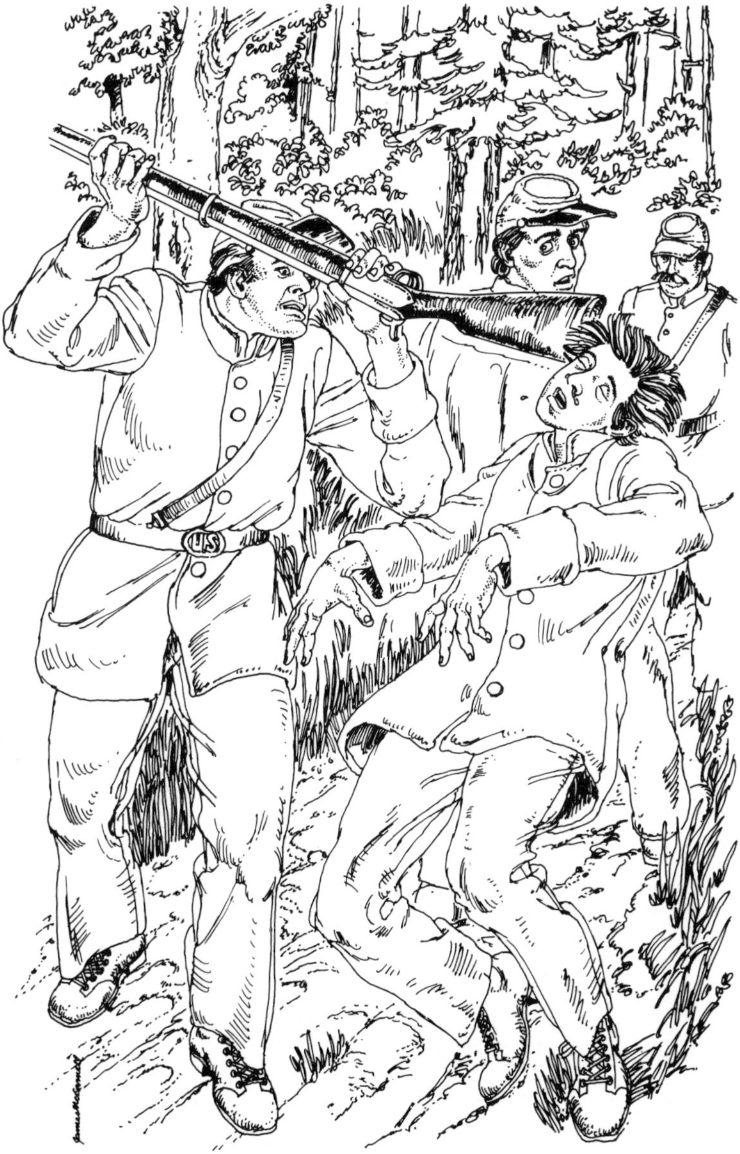

Henry saw a lightning flash before his eyes. Something like a bolt of thunder exploded inside his head. His legs seemed to die as he sank to the ground. Groaning, he tried several times to get up. But each time he fell back, his hands grabbing at the grass.

Finally, with a twisting movement, Henry got up on his hands and knees. Then he managed to get to his feet. Pressing his hands to his head, he went lurching through the grass.

Once he put his hand to the top of his head. He carefully touched the wound. The pain made him draw a long breath through his clenched teeth. His fingers were covered with blood.

The youth walked on in the dusk. The daylight had faded so that he could barely see the ground in front of him. He was afraid to move too quickly because of his wound. He imagined blood flowing slowly down under his hair.

Henry grew more and more weary. His head hung forward, and his shoulders were stooped as if he were carrying a great bundle. His feet shuffled along the ground. He wondered whether he should find a spot on the ground to lie down and sleep.

Just then he heard a cheerful voice say, "You seem to be in a pretty bad way, boy."

The youth did not look up. He just said, "Uh!"

The owner of the cheerful voice took him firmly

by the arm. "Well," he said with a laugh, "I'm going your way. The whole gang is going your way. I guess we can go along together." So they began to walk together like a drunken man and his friend.

As they went along through the dark woods, the man questioned the youth. "What regiment do you belong to? Eh? What's that? The 304th New York? Oh, they're way over in the center, a long way from here. How did you get way over here, anyhow? It will be a miracle if we find our regiments tonight. But I guess we can do it."

The man with the cheerful voice seemed to have an amazing sense of direction. He kept talking as he led the youth through the tangled web of the forest. Often they would meet up with guards and patrols. The man seemed to know just what to say.

At last, the man began to chuckle with glee. "Ah, there you are! See that fire?"

The youth nodded.

"Well, there's where your regiment is. And now, good-bye, old boy. Good luck to you."

The man shook Henry's hand. Then he walked off into the night whistling cheerfully. Henry suddenly realized that he had not once seen the man's face.

Henry walked slowly toward the campfire. He wondered what kind of welcome he would get. He was afraid the men would soon be laughing at him. He had no strength to make up a story.

Suddenly a voice called out, "Halt! Halt!" Henry stood before a rifle barrel that glinted in the firelight. The voice sounded familiar.

Henry called, "Why, hello, Wilson, are you here?"

The rifle was lowered and the loud soldier came forward slowly. He peered into the youth's face. "That you, Henry?"

"Yes, it's . . . it's me," said the youth.

"Well, well, old boy," said the other. "I'm mighty glad to see you. I thought you were dead, sure enough."

Henry could barely stand on his feet. But he wanted to tell his story now, before his comrades could learn the truth. He began, "Yes, I've . . . I've had an awful time. I've been all over. Way over on the right. Terrible fighting over there. I got separated from the regiment. I got shot . . . in the head. I've never seen such fighting."

His friend stepped forward quickly. "What? Got shot? Why didn't you say so right away?"

Another man came up to them. They could see that it was the corporal. "Why, hello, Henry, you here? Why, I thought you were dead! Where were you?"

"Over on the right. I got separated," said the youth.

"Yes, and he got shot in the head. We've got to take care of him," said Wilson.

Wilson and the corporal led Henry over to the fire. Then Wilson went back on guard duty.

"Now, Henry," said the corporal. "Let's have a look at your old head."

The youth sat down. The corporal put down his rifle and began to examine Henry's head. "Ah, here we are! Just as I thought. You've been grazed by a bullet. It's raised a lump just as if someone had hit you on the head with a club. It stopped bleeding a long time ago."

The corporal got up. "By morning your head will feel hot and dry. And you may feel sick. But you'll be OK. Now you just sit here and don't move. I'll send Wilson back here to take care of you." The corporal walked away.

Henry remained on the ground. He stared into the fire. Through the deep shadows he saw that the ground was covered with sleeping men. After a while, Wilson came along. He was carrying two canteens. He gave Henry the canteen with the coffee.

"Well, now, Henry, old boy," said Wilson. "We'll have you fixed up in a minute."

As Henry drank the coffee, Wilson took out a handkerchief. He poured water from the other canteen upon the middle of it. Then he bound the handkerchief over Henry's head. He tied the ends in a knot at the back of Henry's neck.

41

"Well, come on, now. Let's put you to bed and see that you get a good night's rest," said Wilson.

He helped Henry to his feet. Then he led the youth carefully through all the sleeping soldiers who were lying in groups and rows. Soon he stooped and picked up his blankets. He spread the rubber one upon the ground and placed the woolen one about the youth's shoulders.

"There now," Wilson said. "Lie down and get some sleep. You'll feel a whole lot better in the morning."

Henry got down and stretched out. The ground felt soft. Suddenly he said, "Hold on a minute! Where are *you* going to sleep?"

"Right down there next to you," said Wilson. "Now shut up and go to sleep. Don't make a damned fool of yourself."

Henry said no more. As he snuggled down under the blanket, a heavy drowsiness came over him. His head fell forward on his arm and his eyes closed. Hearing a splatter of gunfire in the distance, he wondered if those men ever slept. He gave a long sigh, and in a moment he was asleep.

6 A Second Chance

When Henry awoke, it seemed to him that he had been asleep for a thousand years. An icy dew had chilled his face. He curled further down into his blankets. Gray mists were slowly shifting. Soon the sun would rise and burn the mists away.

Henry stared for a while at the leaves overhead. They were moving in the wind. In the distance he could hear the blaring sounds of fighting. Somehow it seemed that these sounds had no beginning and would never end. All around him were rows and groups of soldiers getting their last moments of sleep. These were the men Henry had dimly seen the night before.

Then Henry heard the noise of a fire crackling in the cold air. Turning his head, he saw his friend Wilson. The loud soldier was putting wood on a small blaze. A few other figures were moving around in the fog. Henry heard the hard cracking of axe blows.

Suddenly there was a hollow rumble of drums. A distant bugle sang faintly. Similar sounds, some softer, some louder, came from near and far over the forest. The bugles called to each other.

There was movement among the men on the ground. Heads lifted up. Much grumbling could be heard as the soldiers dragged themselves awake.

The youth sat up and yawned. "Thunder!" he said, to nobody in particular. He rubbed his eyes. Then he put his hand on his head and carefully felt the bandage over his wound.

Seeing that Henry was awake, his friend came over from the fire. "Well, Henry, old man, how do you feel this morning?" Wilson asked.

The youth yawned again. His head felt like a melon. And there was an unpleasant feeling in his stomach, too. "Oh, Lord, I feel pretty bad," he said.

"I was hoping you'd feel all right this morning. Let's see the bandage—I guess it's slipped," said Wilson. He began to tinker with the bandage in a clumsy way. Finally the youth exploded.

"Gosh darn it," he snapped. "Why can't you be more careful? Now go easy, and don't act as if you were nailing down a carpet."

Henry glared angrily at his friend. But Wilson answered softly, "Well, well, come now, and get some grub. Then, maybe you'll feel better."

At the fireside, the loud soldier watched over his friend's wants with tenderness and care. He poured coffee from a small and sooty tin pail into little black tin cups. Then he roasted some fresh meat on a stick. Finally he sat down and watched Henry eat.

The youth noticed an amazing change in his friend from just the other day. No longer was Wilson a loud soldier. He didn't seem to have a need to swagger and strut anymore. And other people's remarks no longer made him angry. Henry saw that from now on it would be easier to get along with his friend.

Wilson balanced his coffee cup on his knee. "Well, Henry, what do you think our chances are?" he asked. "Will we wipe the Rebels out?"

The youth thought for a moment. "Day before yesterday, you would have bet that you could lick the whole Rebel army all by yourself," he said.

45

His friend looked amazed. "Would I?" he asked. "Well, perhaps I used to think so," he said. He stared at the fire. "I guess I was a pretty big fool then."

After a pause, Wilson continued. "All the officers say we've cornered the Rebs in a tight box. They think we've got them just where we want them."

"I don't know about that," the youth replied. "What I saw over on the right makes me think it was the other way around. From where I was, it looked as if we were getting a good pounding yesterday." Then a sudden thought came to him. "Oh! Jim Conklin's dead."

His friend started. "What? Is he? Jim Conklin?"

The youth spoke slowly. "Yes. He's dead."

"You don't say so. Jim Conklin . . . poor old boy!" There was a long pause. Then Wilson said, "You know, the regiment lost over half its men yesterday. I thought they were all dead. But they kept coming back last night. So it turns out that we only lost a few. They'd been scattered all over. Some of them were wandering around in the woods, fighting with other regiments. Just like you'd done."

"So?" said the youth.

Wilson said nothing. But Henry was worried again. What if Wilson were to question him in more detail about his adventures of the previous day?

Later that morning, the regiment was standing at the side of a lane. The men were waiting for the command to march. Wilson stood next to Henry in the ranks. He was staring down the road. Suddenly he turned to Henry and said, "Fleming!"

"What?" said Henry.

"Well, I guess you might as well give me back those letters," Wilson said.

Henry remembered the yellow packet that Wilson had given him. He remembered how his friend, in a weak moment, had spoken with sobs of his own death. As Henry thought about this, he began to feel superior to Wilson.

"All right, Wilson," said the youth at last. He loosened two buttons of his coat. He thrust in his hand and slowly brought forth the packet. As he held it out to his friend, Wilson's face was turned from him.

Wilson seemed to be suffering great shame. As Henry watched him, he felt his own self-pride and confidence growing. Since nobody knew about his mistakes the day before, he was still a man.

Henry felt pity for Wilson. He thought to himself, "Too bad! The poor devil, it makes him feel bad!" Then Henry remembered how some of the men had run from the battle. As he pictured their terror-struck faces, he felt scorn for them.

Once again, Henry saw himself returning home as a war hero. He would make the hearts of the people glow with his stories of war.

7 "A War Devil"

Henry and the other soldiers in his regiment were on the move again. As they marched, they could hear a constant sputtering of rifle fire. They had been ordered to relieve a command that had been fighting in some damp trenches. When the regiment got there, they took up positions behind a curving line of rifle pits.

The youth leaned against the brown dirt. He looked out at the woods and up and down the line. Curtains of trees blocked his view. On either side of them, guns were roaring without a moment's pause for breath.

Before too long, the regiment was ordered to march again. As they retreated through the woods, they could see the enemy coming after them.

At this sight, Henry exploded in anger. "By God, our general is a lunkhead!" he shouted.

Wilson looked behind them. Then he sighed. "Oh, well, I suppose some of our boys got licked," he said sadly. "Maybe it's not the general's fault. He does the best he can. It's just our luck to get licked often."

Wilson was shuffling along with stooped

shoulders and shifting eyes. He looked like a man who had been whipped and kicked.

"Well, don't we fight like the devil?" asked the youth loudly. He was secretly amazed that he had spoken these words aloud. For a moment Henry lost his courage. He looked about him, but no one questioned his right to say such words. "Don't we do all that men can?" he continued.

In reply, Wilson's voice was stern. "No man will ever dare say we don't fight like the devil. But still, we don't seem to have any luck."

"Well, then, if we fight like the devil and we don't ever win, it must be the general's fault," said Henry. "And I don't see any sense in fighting and fighting if we're always going to lose. And all because of some darned old lunkhead of a general."

A man who was tramping at the youth's side then spoke up. "Maybe you think you fought the whole battle yesterday, Fleming," he said.

"Why, no," said Henry. He cast a frightened glance at the sarcastic man. "I don't think that at all." The youth felt threatened. He became silent.

In a clear space the troops were at last halted. The regiment formed a line facing the enemy infantry. The sun was now directly overhead. As its rays reached down into the gloomy woods, a frenzy of enemy gunfire broke out. The woods began to crackle as if they were on fire.

"I was willing to bet they'd attack as soon as the sun was fairly up," said the lieutenant. In a fit of nerves, he jerked without mercy at his little mustache. He marched back and forth in the rear of his men. The soldiers were lying down behind whatever protection they had collected.

An artillery battery had been moved into position in the rear of Henry's regiment. It began shelling the enemy troops in the distance. The regiment waited with their rifles ready. At any moment, they knew the gray shadows of the woods before them would be slashed by lines of flame. There was much growling and swearing.

"Good God," the youth grumbled. "We're always being chased around like rats! It makes me sick. Nobody seems to know where we go or why we go. I'd like to know why we were marched into these woods, anyhow. Was it just to give the Rebs a regular pot shot at us? Don't tell me it's just luck. I know better. It's the darned old . . ."

Wilson cut in with a calm voice. "It'll turn out all right in the end," he said.

"Oh, the devil it will!" said Henry. "Don't tell me. I know . . ."

"You boys shut right up," cried the lieutenant. "All you've got to do is fight, and there will be plenty of that. Less talking and more fighting is what's best for you boys."

Just then a single rifle flashed in the thicket right before the regiment. In an instant it was joined by many others. The guns in the rear began firing at another band of guns. The battle roar settled to a rolling thunder, which was a single, long explosion.

The men of the regiment watched the advance of the enemy. Some shrank and flinched before the approaching battle.

Henry began to fume with rage. He stamped his foot upon the ground. He scowled with hate at the swirling smoke. How dare the enemy give him no time to rest, no time to sit down and think! Just yesterday he had fought and walked for miles. It had been a long, tiresome adventure. Now he was sore and stiff. He felt he'd earned a rest today.

But those other men, those Rebels, seemed never to grow weary. They were fighting with their usual speed. Henry had a wild hate for the enemy army. He was not going to be treated like a kitten chased by boys. It was not right to drive men into deadly corners. At these moments they could all develop teeth and claws.

He leaned forward and spoke into Wilson's ear. "If they keep on chasing us, by God, they'd better watch out."

His friend twisted his head and made a calm reply. "If they keep on chasing us, they'll drive us all into the river."

The youth cried out savagely at these words. He crouched behind a small tree. His eyes burned with hate, and his mouth set in a snarl. The winds of battle had swept all about the regiment. A dense wall of smoke had settled down. It was slit and slashed by the fire from the rifles.

Henry was not aware that he was standing on his feet and firing his rifle. He lost sense of everything but his hate. The flames bit him, and the hot smoke broiled his skin. His rifle barrel grew so hot that his hands were burning. But he kept on stuffing cartridges and pounding them with his clanking, bending ramrod.

At last the enemy seemed to fall back. The youth went slowly forward, firing his rifle. He aimed at some Rebel soldiers through the smoke. Each time he would pull his trigger with a fierce grunt. It was as if he were striking a blow of his fist with all his strength.

Finally, one by one, all of Henry's comrades had stopped firing. The enemy had indeed fallen back. But Henry was not aware that it was quiet all around him. He kept on firing his rifle.

Someone cried out, "You fool! Don't you know enough to quit when there isn't anything to shoot at? Good God!"

Henry turned then and looked at the blue line of his comrades. They were all staring at him in

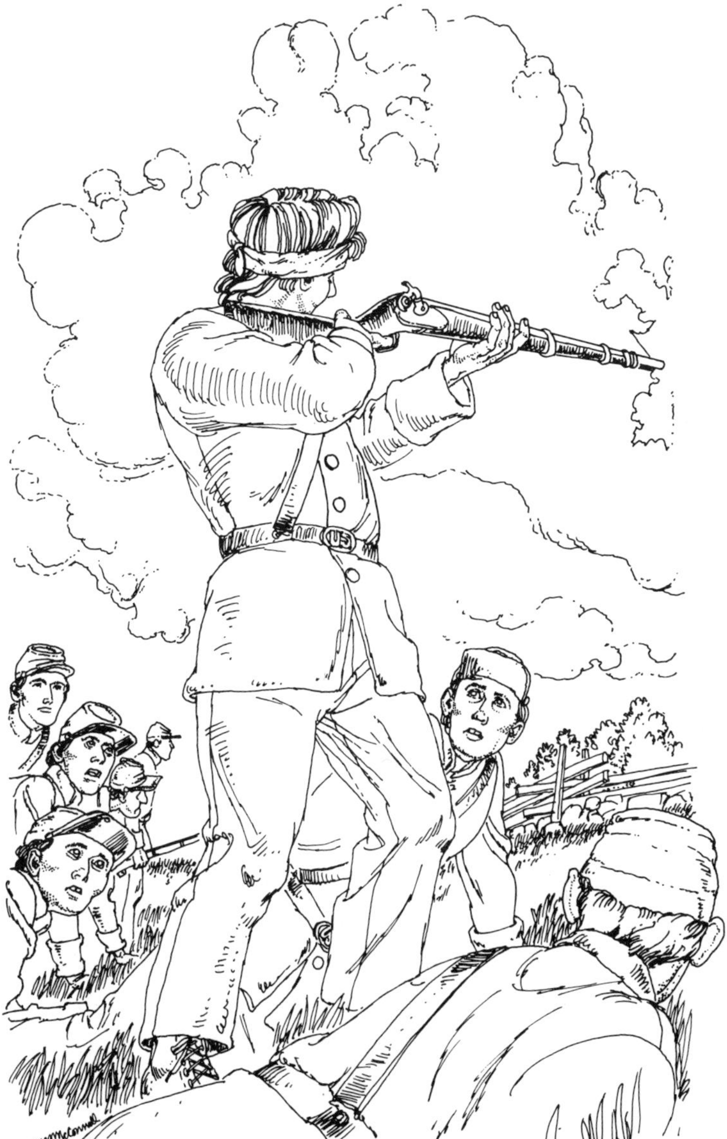
US

amazement. Turning again toward the front, he saw that the enemy soldiers were all gone. He looked confused. Then he suddenly understood and could only say, "Oh."

The youth threw himself upon the ground near his comrades. He sprawled out like a man who had been beaten. His flesh felt as if it were on fire. And the sounds of battle continued in his ears. He groped blindly for his canteen.

The lieutenant was crowing. He seemed drunk with fighting. He called out to the youth: "By heavens, I wish I had ten thousand wild cats like you. Then I could tear the stomach out of this war in less than a week!" He puffed out his chest as he spoke the words.

Some of the men were staring at the youth. He had gone on loading and firing and cursing without a stop. And they had found time to watch him. Now they shook their heads in wonder. "Fleming's a regular war devil," said one of the men.

Wilson came staggering up to him. "Are you all right, Fleming? Do you feel all right? There's nothing the matter with you, is there, Henry?" he said.

"No," said the youth with difficulty. His throat felt sore and tight. He thought about what had just taken place. It seemed that he had fought against tremendous odds. And he had come out of the struggle a hero.

8 "A Lot of Mule Drivers"

One of the men in Henry's regiment had been badly wounded during the fighting. Now he was thrashing about in the grass, twisting his shaking body into strange positions. The man was screaming loudly, crying out for water.

The other soldiers stared at the man. "Who is it?" they asked. "Who is that poor devil?"

"It's Jimmie Rogers. Jimmie Rogers," someone shouted. Nobody made a move to go over to help the man. None of the soldiers had any water left in their canteens.

Wilson thought he knew where a stream was. He got permission to go for some water. Some of the others who saw what Wilson was up to came over to him. They gave him their empty canteens.

"Fill mine, will you?" "Bring me some, too." "And me, too." Wilson left, carrying about a dozen canteens. Henry went with his friend. He felt a strong desire to throw his heated body into the stream. He would soak there and drink quarts of water.

The two friends carefully made their way through the woods. They could hear the sounds of gunfire coming from several different directions. From time to time bullets buzzed in the air and smashed into tree trunks. Some wounded men and other stragglers were also creeping through the woods.

After a while Wilson called a halt. "Henry, I'm afraid I can't find the stream," he said. "I thought it was right around here. We can't spend the rest of the afternoon looking for it. We'll have to go back."

Henry had been looking forward to soaking in the stream. But he had to admit that his friend was right. "Well, I can see there's no water here. Let's head back," he grumbled.

The two friends turned without delay. They began to retrace their steps. As they were passing a clearing, the general in command of their division and his staff rode up. The general almost ran over a wounded man, who was crawling on his hands and knees.

Just then, another officer galloped into the clearing. He reined in his horse just in front of the general.

Henry motioned to his friend to stop. "Let's see if we can hear what they have to say," he whispered. "I think that they're too busy to even notice us."

The general looked at the other officer and spoke coolly. "The enemy is forming over there for another charge," he said. "It'll be directed against

Whiterside. I fear they'll break through there unless we work like thunder to stop them. That means we need to charge the enemy now."

The other swore at his restless horse. Then he cleared his throat. "There will be hell to pay stopping them," he said shortly.

"I suppose so," said the general. Then he began to talk rapidly and in a lower tone. Henry and Wilson could hear nothing until finally the general asked, "What troops can you spare?"

"Well, I had to order in the 12th to help the 76th," the officer said. "And I haven't really got any extra men. But wait, there's the 304th. They fight like a lot of mule drivers. I can spare them best of all."

The youth and his friend looked at each other in astonishment.

The general spoke sharply. "Get them ready, then. I'll watch from here and send you word when to start them. They should be ready to fight in five minutes."

The officer saluted, wheeled around on his horse, and started off. As he rode away, the general called out to him, "I don't believe many of your mule drivers will get back alive."

With terror in their hearts, Henry and Wilson hurried back to their regiment. As the two of them approached the line, the lieutenant saw them. "Fleming, Wilson—how long does it take you to get

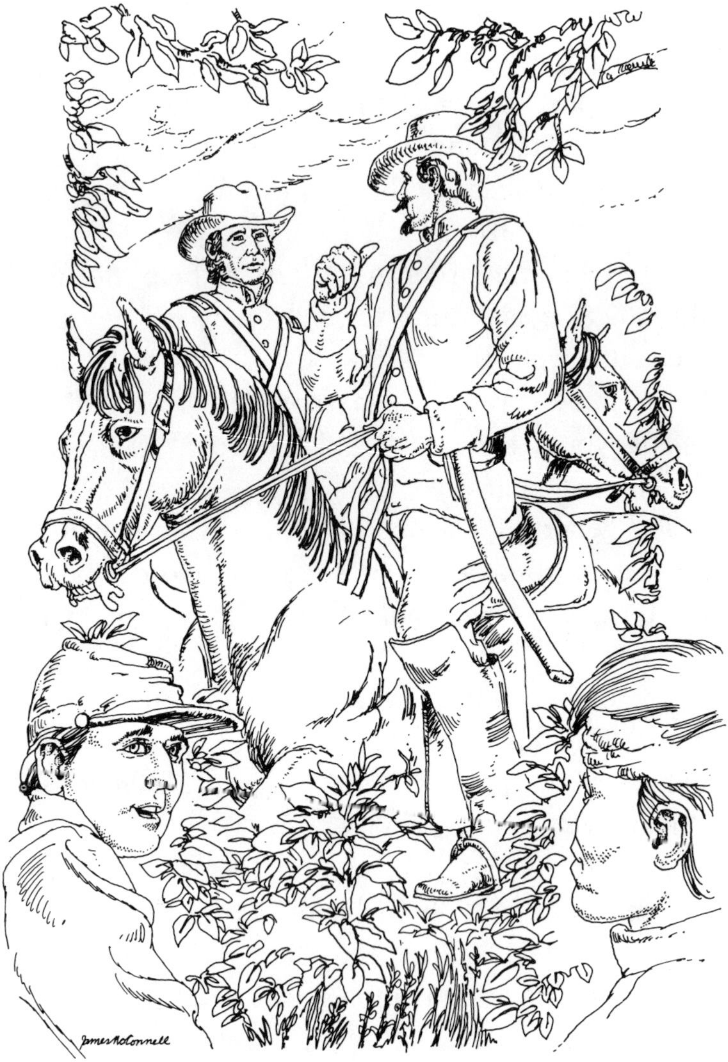
James McConnell

water, anyhow? Where have you been?" he yelled angrily.

"We're going to charge! . . . we're going to charge!" cried Wilson.

"Charge?" said the lieutenant. "Charge? Well, by God. Now, this is real fighting!" A boastful smile lit up his face.

Soon the news spread throughout the regiment. A moment later the officers began to bustle among the men. They pushed the troops into position for the charge. They were like shepherds struggling with sheep.

The youth gave a quick glance at his friend. Their eyes met. Both of them were thinking about the words they had overheard: "Mule drivers . . . hell to pay . . . don't believe many will get back alive." They both nodded in agreement when a shaggy man near them said, "We'll get swallowed."

From the corners of his eyes, Henry saw an officer come galloping up, waving his hat. Suddenly Henry felt a straining and heaving among the men. The line fell slowly forward like a wall toppling. The youth was pushed and jostled for a moment. Then he lunged ahead and began to run.

As he ran, Henry fixed his eye upon a distant clump of trees. He had decided that this is where the enemy would be met. Now he ran toward it as if toward a goal.

When the regiment swung from its position into a clearing, the woods seemed to come alive. Yellow flames shot out from many directions. The line of soldiers lurched straight for a moment. Then the right wing sprang forward, and then the left wing.

The youth ran in advance of the line. His eyes were still fixed on the clump of trees. The wild yells of the Rebels could be heard coming from the woods.

The terrible song of bullets was in the air. Shells snarled among the treetops. One fell into the middle of a group of men and exploded in fury. Still the regiment rushed forward in a frenzy. The men were cheering and shouting madly as they ran. Many were hit by bullets and fell to the ground. The regiment was leaving a trail of bodies.

Finally the charge ran out of steam. The leaders began to slacken the pace. The men began to notice that their comrades were dropping with moans and shrieks. The regiment stopped its advance.

Now the sputter of gunfire from the woods became a steady roar. Above this noise the men heard the shouting of the lieutenant. "Come on, you fools!" he yelled. His face was black with rage. "Keep going! You can't stay here."

The men stared blankly at the lieutenant who stood, cursing and screaming, with his back to the enemy. Suddenly, Wilson sprang to life. He lurched forward. Dropping to his knees, he fired an angry shot at the enemy.

This action awakened the men. Once more, the regiment began to move forward slowly. But the men halted again when they reached the edge of an open field.

Again the lieutenant began to yell and swear at his men. He grabbed Henry by the arm. "Come on, you lunkhead!" he roared. "We'll all get killed if we stay here. We've only got to cross that field. And then . . . " The rest of his idea disappeared in a blue haze of curses.

"Cross there?" said Henry.

"Just cross the field. We can't stay here," screamed the lieutenant. He was still grasping Henry's arm, and he now began to drag the youth.

Henry felt a sudden anger at the lieutenant, and shook him off. "Come on yourself, then," he yelled in a bitter voice. They both ran along the front line of the regiment. Wilson ran after them.

The three men stopped in front of the flag. "Come on! Come on!" they yelled. The flag swept toward them. And the regiment once again surged forward.

Over the field went the scurrying soldiers. The youth ran like a madman to reach the woods before a bullet could find him. He ducked his head low and nearly closed his eyes as he ran. The scene was a wild blur.

Henry kept close to the color sergeant, the man carrying the flag. Somehow Henry felt drawn to the flag. It seemed that no harm could come to it. And the flag, he felt, had the power to save lives.

Suddenly, Henry became aware that the color sergeant had been hit and had gone down. Henry sprang for the flagpole and clutched at it. At the same instant, Wilson grabbed it from the other side.

Both men jerked at the flagpole. But the color sergeant was dead, and the corpse would not let go of the flag. Finally they pulled it away from the dead man. Now Henry and Wilson struggled over the flag. Finally, Henry pushed his friend away.

When the two friends looked around, they saw that the regiment was in retreat again. The men were headed back toward the trees. "There go the mule drivers!" said Henry with a scowl of rage. Maybe that officer was right after all!

When Henry and Wilson caught up with the regiment, the officers were screaming at the men again. The lieutenant had been shot in the arm. It hung at his side, useless. But this didn't stop him from cursing.

Henry was almost out of his mind with rage. "So we're no better than mule drivers, are we?" he thought to himself. He ran up and down the regiment, holding the flag high. He added his own loud curses to those of the lieutenant. He tried to drag some of the men forward. But it was no use. The regiment was like a machine that had worn down.

Henry and the lieutenant continued to scold the men. Then suddenly a fresh wave of enemy soldiers sprang from the trees. All of them were yelling and running toward the regiment. Henry's comrades seemed about to panic.

Wilson ran up to Henry. "Well, Henry, I guess this is good-bye," he said.

"Oh, shut up, you damned fool!" said Henry. He stood his ground in the midst of the confused soldiers, holding the flag steady in his hand.

Now the officers began to quickly push the men into a proper circle to face the enemy. The soldiers fell to the ground and took cover as best they could.

The lieutenant cried out, "Here they come! Right on to us, by God!" The rest of his words were lost in the roar of the men's rifles.

Henry sat on the ground with his flag between his knees. He could see the Rebels in their light gray uniforms coming forward through the smoke. They got so close that Henry could see the features of their faces.

Angry rifle fire crackled back and forth between the men in blue and the men in gray. Soon there was so much smoke in the air that it was hard to see anything.

Finally the fighting slowed down. Fewer bullets ripped the air. Then it was quiet. When the smoke lifted, it became clear that the enemy had retreated. The Rebels had lost many men. A cheer went up from the men in blue.

As the men were resting on the grass, an officer came galloping along the line. It was the officer who had called the men "mule drivers." He stopped in front of the colonel.

"What an awful mess you made!" he shouted angrily. "Good Lord, man, if your men had gone a hundred feet farther, you would have made a great charge. But as it is . . ."

The colonel shrugged his shoulders. "Oh, well, Sir, we went as far as we could," he said calmly.

"As far as you could? Did you, by God?" snorted the other. "Well, that wasn't very far, was it?" he said coldly. He wheeled his horse and rode stiffly away.

The lieutenant said to the colonel, "If any man says these boys didn't put up a good fight out there, he's a damned fool."

"Lieutenant," began the colonel, "this is my own affair, and I'll trouble you . . ."

"All right, colonel, all right," said the lieutenant.

News of the officer's remarks passed along the line. It made the men angry. Wilson said, "Does he think we went out there and played marbles? I've never heard of such a thing!"

"Oh, well," said Henry, "he probably didn't see any of it at all. He only got mad because we didn't do what he wanted done. It's just our bad luck, that's all."

"I should say so," said Wilson.

Just then several men came rushing up to Henry and his friend. "Fleming, you should have heard!" cried one of the men.

"Heard what?" said the youth.

"Well, we heard the colonel and the lieutenant talking. The colonel wanted to know who carried the flag. When the lieutenant said 'Fleming,' the colonel said, 'He's a very good man to have. He kept the flag way in the front.' 'You bet,' said the lieutenant. 'He and a fellow named Wilson were at the head of the charge.' 'Well, well,' said the colonel, 'they deserve to be major-generals.' "

Henry and Wilson gave each other a secret glance of joy. Their faces were flushed with pleasure. They quickly forgot many things—things that had made them feel bad. At this moment they were very happy men.

9 Victory

Once again, enemy troops began to pour forth from the woods. Now Henry was full of self-confidence. He stood tall and calm. He looked at the line of troops that formed a blue curve along the side of a hill. He watched the attack begin against a part of the line. He smiled when he saw men dodge the shells that were thrown at them.

The youth stood still as he viewed the scene. He still held the flag. But he seemed to have forgotten that he also had a role to play. For the moment he was too busy watching the others. The crash and swing of the great drama made him lean forward. He was not even aware of his breathing. The flag hung silently over him.

A line of the enemy came within dangerous range. The Rebel soldiers could be seen clearly—tall, gaunt men with excited faces. They were running with long strides toward a fence.

At the sight of this danger, Henry's comrades threw up their rifles and fired a volley at the enemy. There had been no order given. The men had immediately sent forth their flock of bullets without waiting for a command.

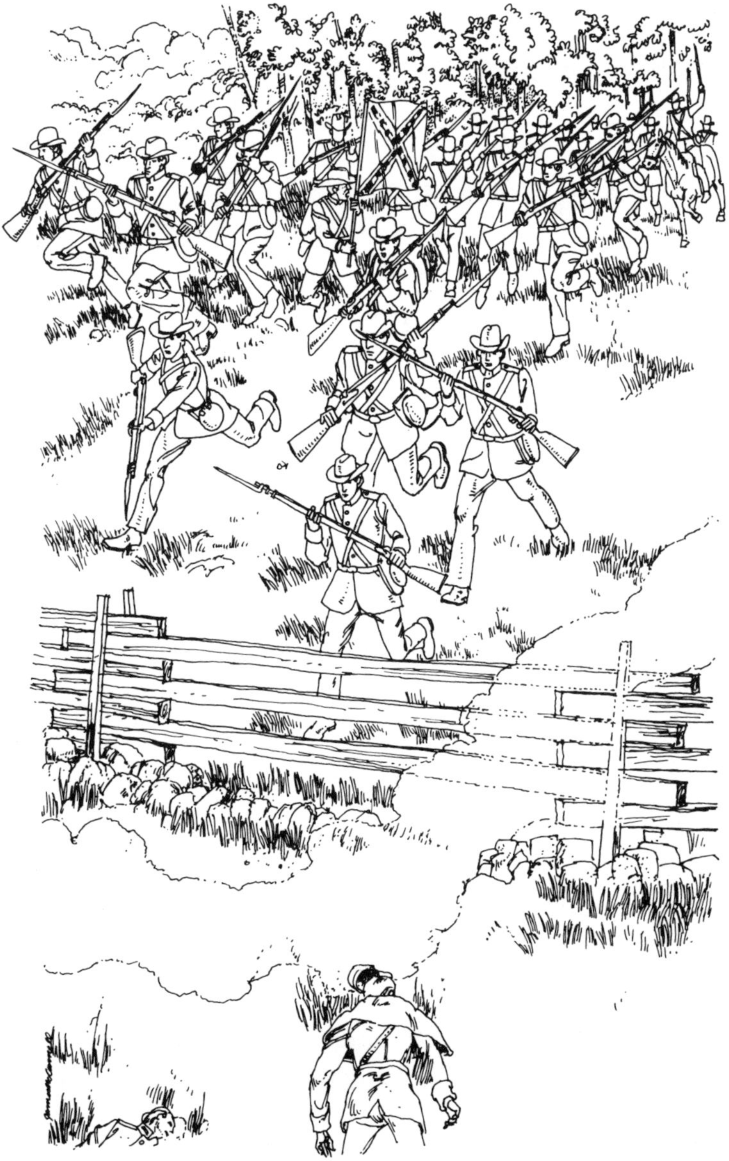

But the enemy soldiers were quick to gain the protection of the fence. They slid down behind it. From this position, they began to slice up the men in blue.

Henry's regiment began to take new losses. One after another, grunting bundles of blue dropped to the ground. The orderly sergeant was shot through the cheeks. His jaw hung down, showing a mass of blood and broken teeth in the wide opening of his mouth. He tried to cry out for help and ran off to the rear of the line.

Others fell down around the feet of their companions. Some of the wounded crawled out and away. But many lay still, their bodies twisted into impossible shapes.

The youth saw the lieutenant holding a position in the rear. The man continued to swear at his troops. But now it was with the air of a man who was using his last box of curses.

The colonel came running along the back of the line. There were other officers following him. "We must charge them!" they shouted. "We must charge them!" they cried with angry voices. They seemed to be afraid that the men might not obey their orders.

Henry studied the distance between him and the enemy. He saw that his regiment would have to go forward. It would be death to stay where they were.

Their best hope was to push the enemy away from the fence.

The men of the regiment seemed to agree. At the shouted words of command, the soldiers sprang forward. They bolted ahead in eager leaps. It was as if they knew that this was a last burst of energy. It was as if they had agreed to get the job done quickly so they could go on living.

The blind rush carried the men in dusty and tattered blue across the field toward the fence. From behind the fence the rifles of the enemy kept on sputtering.

The youth kept the bright flag to the front. He was waving his free arm in circles, shrieking madly as he ran. It seemed that the mob of men in blue were growing wild as they hurled themselves forward. They were in a state of frenzy, shouting and cheering. This made Henry run even faster. Now he thought of the bullets only as things that could stop him from reaching the fence.

As the regiment moved ahead, Henry saw that many of the men in gray were retreating. Some of them turned now and then to fire at the advancing blue wave. Just one part of the Rebel line was held by a grim and stubborn group. They stood their ground. Most of them were settled firmly down behind fence posts and rails. Their flag waved over them while their rifles fired fiercely.

The men in blue were now very close to the men in gray. Both groups began to shout insults at each other. Those in blue showed their teeth; their eyes were wide and shone all white.

The youth had fixed his gaze on the Rebel flag. He plunged like a mad horse at it. He would not let it escape him if wild blows could seize it. His own flag was winging toward the other.

The men in blue came to a sudden halt at close range. They roared a swift volley. The group in gray was split and broken by this fire. But still they fought. The men in blue yelled again and rushed in upon them.

Henry saw several men stretched upon the ground. Standing among them was the man carrying the Rebel flag. He had been hit and was having trouble staying on his feet. The look of death was on his face. He held onto the flag and staggered backward away from the fence.

Wilson leaped over the fence and sprang at the Rebel flag. He pulled at it and grabbed it away from the wounded man with a mad cry. The Rebel soldier, gasping, lurched over and fell down. His dead face was turned to the ground. There was a pool of blood on the grass under his head.

Henry's regiment broke out into wild cheers. Those who still had hats or caps threw them high into the air.

At one part of the line, four enemy soldiers had been taken prisoner. One of the prisoners had been wounded in the foot. He cursed at his captors. Another prisoner, a young boy, was calm and good natured. He was quite willing to talk about the battle with the Union soldiers.

The third prisoner coldly answered any question with, "Ah, go to hell!" And the fourth prisoner said nothing. He acted as if he were ashamed to have been captured.

After the men had celebrated enough, they settled down behind the fence. Since there was some tall grass there, Henry stretched out and rested in it. He leaned his flag against the fence.

Wilson came to him there. He was holding his treasure—the Rebel flag. The two weary men sat side by side and congratulated each other.

10 Glad to Be Alive

The roar of the gunfire slowly died away. The rifles were silent. Every now and then the boom of artillery could be heard in the distance. Otherwise it was quiet on the battlefield.

The youth stood up. He shaded his eyes with his grimy hand and gazed over the field. "Well, what now, I wonder?" he said.

His friend also rose and said. "I bet we're going to get along out of here and back over the river."

They waited, watching. Within an hour the regiment received orders to retrace its way. The men grunted as they got up from the grass. They shook their tired legs, and stretched their arms over their heads. One man swore as he rubbed his eyes. They all groaned, "Oh, Lord!"

The men moved slowly back across the field. They kept on marching until they had joined the other regiments of the brigade. The soldiers now marched in a long column through the woods. Finally they reached the road.

At this point the brigade curved away from the woods across a field. The column of soldiers went winding off in the direction of the river. Henry turned his head and looked over his shoulder. Then he said to his friend, "Well, it's all over."

Wilson gazed backward. "By God, it is," he agreed. Through Henry's mind flashed pictures of all that had happened in the past two days. He kept seeing again the enemy soldiers charging at him. He remembered the roar of the guns and the bullets whizzing by him. He could still hear the shells that had exploded near him.

The longer Henry thought about it, the more amazed he was. Here he was, walking along, talking, breathing. He was still alive. The battle was over, and he had come through it alive. This thought filled him with happiness.

Suddenly Wilson cried, "Good Lord!"

"What?" asked the youth.

"Good Lord!" repeated his friend. "You know Jimmie Rogers? You remember when he was hurt and we tried to find some water for him? Well, he— gosh, I haven't seen him since then. Say, has anybody seen Jimmie Rogers?"

"Seen him? No! He's dead," said the soldier marching in back of Wilson.

Wilson swore. The men kept marching.

Henry began to think about everything he had done. He remembered his brave deeds and thought about the praise he'd received. He was proud of himself.

But then he reminded himself of his failures. Why had he fled from that first battle? He knew he was not a coward. He must have run because he didn't know any better. Yet he felt ashamed.

Henry felt even greater shame when he remembered the tattered soldier who had needed his help. He had left the poor man to die alone in the field. Could he ever forgive himself? He broke out in a chill of sweat and swore out loud.

Wilson turned to him. "What's the matter, Henry?" he asked. The youth's reply was an outburst of curses.

Henry was going over each detail of the scene

with the tattered soldier. Finally he calmed down. He knew that he couldn't change the past. Perhaps such a great mistake could be useful to him. It might teach him to see things in balance. There was no need for him to feel too guilty nor too proud. He need not be loud or boastful. He was but a man, after all.

It began to rain. The column of weary soldiers marched through a sea of liquid brown mud. The men were muttering and swearing. Yet the youth smiled. He saw that he was going to be all right. He had rid himself of the sickness of battle. The nightmare, the heat and pain of war, was in the past.

Over the river a golden ray of sun came through the dark rain clouds.